Launch your kids into the wowza world of
author/illustrator Courtney Watkins's creativity!
Kids will revel in the dynamic, big-thinking,
get-moving possibilities on every page!

DREAM IT!
DRAW IT!
THINK IT!
DO IT!

Activities to Ignite Creativity

COURTNEY WATKINS

Andrews McMeel Publishing®

a division of Andrews McMeel Universal

ALERT!
COMBUSTIBLE CONTENTS

able to explode

This book contains WOWZA, wackadoodle, funny, brain-bending IDEAS that will definitely ignite YOUR CREATIVITY!

Get ready...

checklist:
- ☐ Pen
- ☐ Colored Pencils
- ☐ Markers
- ☐ Wit (humor)
- ☐ Wits (mind)
- ☐ Helmet (for page 8)

Get set...

Write your full name: _Elise victoria tabb_

What do you like to be called? _Elise_

How would you describe yourself?
- ☐ amazing
- ☐ hilarious
- ☐ athletic
- ☑ peaceful
- ☑ bright
- ☑ kind
- ☑ curious
- ☐ powerful
- ☑ _____ OTHER
- ☐ inventive
- ☑ strong
- ☑ helpful
- ☑ _____ OTHER

And how would you describe yesterday's lunch?
- ☑ crunchy
- ☐ hot
- ☑ heathy
- ☐ needed more ketchup
- ☑ soft
- ☐ cold
- ☐ noodle-y
- ☐ _____ OTHER

Check your watch... it's spontaneous quote time!

"Nothing would delight me more than a trip to...

france in _Winter_ !
   CITY OR PLACE   SEASON

I'd like to go with _Arr & Katie_.

I'll be sure to pack _fancy Dress_,

fancy shoes & _Brush_.

And I'm not coming home 'til I get a great shot of

the french Backery !

Add details to show if this is a rabbit or a bird.

And you can quote me on that!"

1

Scavenger Hunt: Anywhere

Look for an object that matches the description.
Write down what you find and X what it can fit in.

It can fit in a...

✓ when you see it	DESCRIPTION	What is it?	hand	treasure chest	train car
☑	fuzzy	Rug	☐	☐	☑
☑	blue	Shirt	☐	☑	☑
☑	striped	~~Pant~~ Pants	☐	☑	☑
☑	pointed	~~Sci~~ pencil	☑	☑	☑
☑	unusual	mose chran	☑	☑	☑
☑	wooden	cabens	☐	☐	☑
☑	rough	Book	☐	☑	☑
☑	shiny	glassdoor	☐	☐	☑
☑	clear	Water Bottle	☐	☑	☑
☑	metal	Lights	☐	☑	☑
☑	beautiful	mom	☐	☐	☑

WHAT? Where? WHY?
Add details to answer these Qs!

Uh-oh!

Color Me Bright

Fill the square with your favorite shade of each color.
Name it. Be specific! "Dandelion Yellow" "Licorice Red"

COLOR:

How does it make you feel?:

Red

twizzer red
SPECIFIC NAME

☐ Tingly   ☑ Angry

☐ Powerful   ☐ Hot

☐ _____
OTHER

Orange

warm orange
SPECIFIC NAME

☐ Friendly   ☐ Scared

☐ Courageous   ☑ Warm

☐ _____
OTHER

Yellow

Sunflower yellow
SPECIFIC NAME

☑ Happy   ☐ Seasick

☐ Creative   ☐ Hopeful

☐ _____
OTHER

Pink

Sweet pink
SPECIFIC NAME

☑ Sweet ☐ Tired
☐ Healthy ☐ Content
☐ _____
                OTHER

Gold

royal gold
SPECIFIC NAME

☐ Safe ☐ Greedy
☐ Capable ☑ Royal
☐ _____
                OTHER

Write your name in a fancy way using all of these colors!

Elisee

Change your mood by changing the colors around and on you.

NEW Product for the Shower!

What is it? Name it. Label it. Rave about it.

lazy marc's hair poofer!

CAUTION:
If you are 3 or younger do not use.

Rave Review:

"Wowee! Ever since I started using ___lazy marc's hair poofer___
NAME OF PRODUCT

my ☐toes ☐ears ☑hands ☐eyebrows ☑ __feet__
OTHER

are ☐shinier ☐twice as long ☐green ☐ __Softer__ ".
OTHER

6

"¿Cuántos años tiene su gato guapo?"

/ Kwawn·toes   an·yoes   T·N·A   soo gaw·toe gwaw·poe/

That's SPANISH for: "How old is your handsome cat?"

DRIVER's LICENSE

☆ Select your wheels:

☒ scooter ☐ bike ☐ rollerblades ☐ cart ☐ _____ OTHER

☆ Picture of YOU!

Your Whole Name: Elisa victoria Tabb

Address: 241 West Berkswell Dr.

Birthday: ~~April~~ April, 26th

☆ Design your helmet!
• Choose 2 main colors:
Pink
Purple

• Create a symbol like:
⚡ ☮ ➡ 🐝

☆ Select Speed Level:
☐ Plodding Turtle   ☐ Olympic Sprinter   ☐ Speed-Walking Neighbor Lady
☐ Rushing Squirrel ☑ NASA Rocket   ☐ _____ OTHER

☆ Preferred Course:
☐ Sidewalk   ☐ Grocery Aisle   ☐ Driveway   ☐ School Hallway
☐ Playground ☑ Road   ☐ Carpet in Library ☐ _____ OTHER

☆ FaNcy SIGNATURE: Elise Tabb

CAUTION! Entering the territory of a made-up word:

PERSONimate

Personify + Animate

Give human
characteristics
to an object

Make
something
move

Now that you know that... Personimate this:

Six Pears Dancing!

UnDOODLE it

Turn these doodles into different drawings.

Picture This

"A SCIAPODOUS gardener GALUMPHING"

⇩
/sigh-ap-uh-dass/
having very large feet

⇩
/ga-lum-fing/
moving in a loud
and clumsy way

Now draw it!

AGILITY COURSE

→ OUTSIDE ←

Agility is the ability to move quickly and easily!

Design an obstacle course to test your agility.

You may wish to include some of these objects in your design:

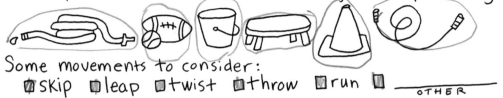

Some movements to consider:

☑ skip ☑ leap ☑ twist ☑ throw ☑ run ☑ _____ OTHER

START

Leap 3 times

three time leap

Spray the cyana

land in the Bush

Jump the River

Now go set it up
for REAL!
Time yourself!
Challenge a buddy!
Race backward!

Boomerang: Person

What goes around comes around.
So, throw a KINDNESS out there and see what happens!

Your Mission: Think of something Terrific you can do for someone.

Target: ___Rebeca___

Name of Person

What will you do?
☑ Help out ☐ Cheer up ☐ Entertain ☐ Other: _____

Details of your Idea: _____

_____

_____

When will this happen?   Where?
___Jan. 5TH___   ___Play Date___
Needed Supplies: _yes_   Helpers: _Madonson_

_____   _____

_____   _____

Your Results: How'd it go?
☐ Even better than I imagined!!! ☐ GREAT! ☐ Pretty Good!
Explain: _____

_____

How do you feel? ☐😃 ☑☮ ☐⚡ ☐♡

14

Drawing with Letters

Draw a pug from C,O,V. "Ruff?" Go ahead and try it!

Trick Question:
How do you spell
PUG?
CCCCOOOV
Get it?

"Qu'est-ce que c'est?"
/KESS KUH SAY/
That's FRENCH for "What is it?"!

It's a drawer missing a knob.

It's a Hula-Hoop left on the playground.

It's a slice of lazy Swiss cheese.

It's _____

It's _____

It's _____

It's _____

Ask friends! Fill in their answers below:

It's _____

It's _____

So then...
Qu'est-ce que c'est?

16

Rippling

"Kindly finish the pattern I've started until it fills the box!"

Which-a-Wayer

Stand up. Walk 5 steps in any direction.
Close your eyes. Turn to the left.
Open your eyes. Draw what you see.

Drawing with NUMBERS:

Draw a pastry chef from 2,3,5,7,8. "Donut dare?" Go ahead and try it!

How come the pastry chef's watch runs slow?
Because it always goes back four seconds!

Get it?

AWESOME...
is going on vacation!

For the next two weeks you must use other words to express "Awesome!"

Add to the wall of awesome possibilities!

AMAZING

fantastic ♡

delightful ☺

⭐STELLAR⭐

'Bye! Hope your trip is...

Don't say it!

AWESOME

CHALLENGE A FRIEND TO DO THE SAME

FOR YOU! ✭POETRY SLAM⚡

Seemingly NONSENSE but somehow makes so much sense!

1. Choose a plant:

☐ daisy ☑ palm tree ☐ cactus

☐ _____
OTHER

2. Describe your choice in 5 words and write them on the numbered lines.

✭ Attention!:
   Do not use the word "green."

Now, let's make this INTERESTING!

3. Choose a BOLD and completely unrelated word:

☑ Pride ☐ Humanity ☐ Midnight

☐ _____
OTHER

4. Write your choice TWICE - on the top and bottom wavy lines.

5. Have a friend do the very same thing on the next page.

✭ Attention!:
   Do not show your poem yet!

1 _____

2 _____

3 _____

4 _____

5 _____

For a FRIEND! ⚡ Poetry Slam ⚡

Seemingly NONSENSE but somehow makes so much sense!

1. Choose a plant:

☐ daisy ☐ palm tree ☐ cactus

☐ _____
   OTHER

2. Describe your choice in 5 words and write them on the numbered lines.
⭐ Attention!:
   Do not use the word "green."

Now, let's make this INTERESTING!

3. Choose a BOLD and completely unrelated word:

☐ Pride ☐ Humanity ☐ Midnight

☐ _____
   OTHER

4. Write your choice TWICE - on the top and bottom wavy lines.

5. Gather an audience and take turns reading your poems out loud and with STYLE! Use rhythm, rap, jazz!

1 _____
2 _____
3 _____
4 _____
5 _____

What's on the Surface?

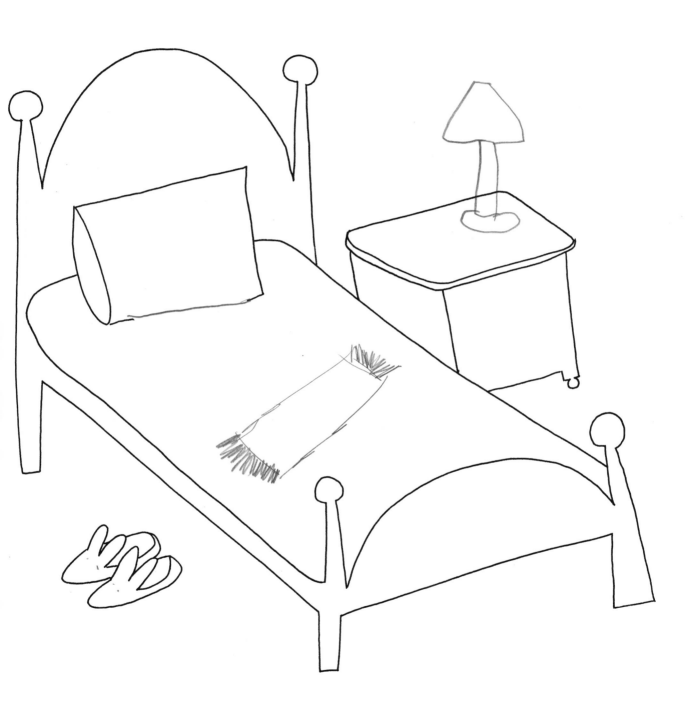

Grasshoppering!

Jumping from one random idea to another.

A mystery guest is coming to your house! You hope it's

___a friend___ because ___your bored___
NAME OF PERSON

___and you wan to hang out today___.

What do you imagine penguins think about? _____
___Swimming, playing around in the snow,___
___eating fish, putting on a show___.

In 30 years, you'll be famous for ___danceing or___
___Singing___
_____

☆ Make a choice and then ask yourself, "Why?" ☆

☐ treehouse or ☑ castle   ☑ 4th of July or ☐ Thanksgiving
☐ whispering or ☑ yelling   ☐ Inventing or ☑ Collecting
☑ rock star or ☐ scientist   ☑ Speaking French or ☐ Speaking Dog

Give a friend these options and be sure to ask, "Why?"!

Besides flossing, think of 3 other uses for dental floss:
1. ___String___
2. ___rope___
3. ___chain___

The Penguin in My Room

NEW Product for the House!

What is it? Name it. Label it. Rave about it.

magic cleaner ☆

Guaranteed to:

Clean up faster than ever

Rave Review:

"Yeah! My ☐dining room ☐hallway ☑bedroom ☐ _____ OTHER
is now ☐brighter ☐cozier ☐tidier ☑ cleaner _____ OTHER
because _of the magic cleaner_ ."

Create a CRITTER

Go into your BEDROOM. Find something blue that will fit on this page. Trace around it. Now turn the shape into a FEROCIOUS critter.

Three Wishes

Digging in the sand, you discover a genie lamp!

Notice the intricate design (hint-hint)

The genie pops out offering you a selection of wishes.
You may choose 3: ☑ a horse ☐ good health ☐ an adventure
☐ world peace ☐ a helicopter ☑ $500 ☐ genius IQ ☑ a dog
☐ a cure for _____ ☐ tiger-like strength

Of your 3 choices, select 1 and "anchor" it. In other words, → YOU take charge of making a wish come true!

_____

_____

_____

_____ .

Drawing with Letters:

Draw a horse from M, C, J, L, O. "Neigh?" Go ahead and try it!

For good luck, always hold a horseshoe <u>UP</u> like a "U"!

Scavenger Hunt: Outside

Look for an object that matches the description.
Write down what you find and X what it can fit in.

It can fit in a...

✓ when you see it	DESCRIPTION	What is it?	hand	treasure chest	train car
☐	red	Car	☐	☒	☑
☐	huge	Spider	☐	☑	☐
☐	delicate	ring	☑	☐	☐
☐	curved	string	☐	☑	☐
☐	bug-bitten	roach	☑	☐	☐
☐	surprising	present	☐	☑	☐
☐	iridescent [0]	Scented tree	☑	☐	☐
☐	sharp	pencil	☑	☐	☐
☐	brand new	Shirt	☐	☑	☐
☐	round	Ball	☐	☑	☐

[0] having colors that seem to change when seen from different angles

CAUTION! Entering the territory of a made-up word:

PERSONimate

Personify + Animate

Give human
characteristics
to an object

Make
something
move

Now that you know that... Personimate this:

Two Chairs Ice-Skating

♪ My Song ♪♪♪

Using a pencil, draw dots on the lines and spaces below.

Now, play your song on any keyboard.
Or ask someone to play it for you!
How does it sound? If you hear any wonky notes,
simply erase that dot and place it somewhere else!

WHAT? Where? WHY?
Add details to answer these Qs!

Boomerang: Animal

What goes around comes around.
So, throw a **KINDNESS** out there and see what happens!

Your Mission: Think of something **NICE** you can do for an animal!

Target: __Brownie__   ☑Pet ☐Wild
Name of Animal

What will you do?
☐Feed ☐Train ☑Exercise ☐Surprise ☐ _____ _other_

Details of your Idea: _____
_____
_____

When will this happen?   Where?
_____   _____

Needed Supplies: _____ Helpers: _____
_____   _____
_____   _____

Your Results: How'd it go?
☐Even better than I imagined!!! ☐GREAT! ☐Pretty Good!
Explain: _____
_____

How do you feel? ☐😺 ☐🐶 ☐☺ ☐ _____ _other_

Rippling

"Please continue my pattern to the edges of the page!"

Which-a-Wayer

Turn to your right. Walk to the closest object.
Introduce yourself! Gather the following info:

Object's Name: _____

Object's Purpose: _____

Object's Origin: _____

Object's Weight: _____

Height: _____

Width: _____

Object's Portrait

Ideas for improving this object:

☐ New Shape   ☐ New Size

☐ New Color   ☐ _____
OTHER

Elaborate (Give details) here:

_____

_____

_____

_____.

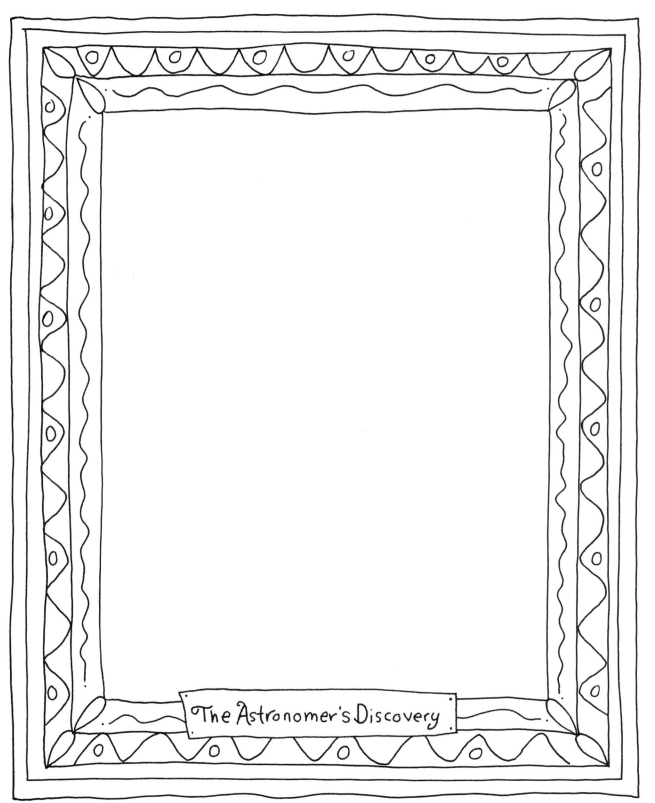

The Astronomer's Discovery

PAIR

Two matching shoes are called a pair.
Draw pairs of shoes that are perfect for...

Hiking	A Party	Running

Other things that come in pairs are...

socks	mittens	earrings	dice

"Pair" is also used for objects that have two parts joined together.

If that's the case, why not call me a pair of shirt?

Now draw a pair of parrots paring pears in paradise.

What's on the Surface?

◁Ec•d⤙e

Unravel the code on the left by reading it out loud.
Decode it by holding up the translation to a mirror.

Code	→Translation←

Tranquil train call
Ladles czar
Hawaii under wet chew art
Upper butter whirled sew eye
Lie could almond hen disguise

(mirror text)
Twinkle, twinkle,
little star,
How I wonder what you are.
Up above the world so high,
Like a diamond in the sky.

Decode these lines with a friend taking turns
reading them out loud. Can you hear it?

Code	→Translation←

Hippie bird hay! _____

Olive hue! _____

Watts 14 her? _____

Boot Eiffel wetter wire heaven. _____

Watching aim? _____

Y, 10 Q! _____

All of some her! _____

(mirror text)
Beautiful weather we're having. Why, thank you! Love summer!
Happy Birthday! Love you! What's for dinner; What's your name;

Create a CRITTER

Go into the KITCHEN. Choose a gadget that will fit on this page. Trace around it. Now turn the shape into a friendly critter.

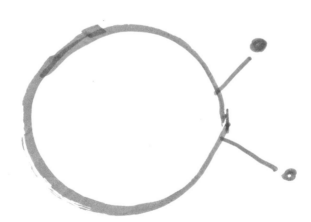

Color Me Cool

Fill the square with your favorite shade of each color.
Name it. Be specific! "Dragon Scale Purple," "Noon Sky Blue"

COLOR:

Green

ocean green
SPECIFIC NAME

How does it make you feel?:

☐ Fresh ☐ Jealous
☑ Motivated ☐ Healthy
☐ _____
OTHER

Blue

moon Blue
SPECIFIC NAME

☐ Peaceful ☑ Sad
☐ Smart ☐ Mellow
☐ _____
OTHER

Purple

Dragon purple
SPECIFIC NAME

☑ Dreamy ☐ Grumpy
☐ Energized ☐ Calm
☐ _____
OTHER

Black

Dark Sky Black
SPECIFIC NAME

☐ Mysterious ☐ Strange
☑ Dramatic ☐ Upset
☐ _____
                OTHER

Silver

fog silver
SPECIFIC NAME

☐ Puzzled ☐ Cold
☐ Capable ☑ Mighty
☐ _____
                OTHER

Write your initials in a COOL way using all of these colors!

ETV

Choose how you want to feel. Surround yourself with that color.

Greeting a Dog

As you may know, it's customary and quite necessary to let a dog sniff your hand when you're first meeting.

See what happens when you bring this page right up to your eyes!

Now that the dog has had a good sniff, she knows you're a "Good-o!" And she knows...

...what you've eaten for breakfast:
□ cereal □ a banana ☑ sausage □ _____
                                              OTHER

...if you have any pets:
□ Yes, I have _____.
                        LIST YOUR PETS
☑ No, but I did pet ___Dogs_____.
                        LIST ANIMALS PETTED

...if you've brushed your teeth. (Well, maybe not. But have you?)
☑ Yes!   □ I never forget because
□ I will now.   I don't want dog breath!

44

FOR YOU! ☆ POETRY SLAM

Seemingly NONSENSE but Somehow makes so much sense!

1. Choose an animal

☐ mosquito   ☐ moose   ☑ hedge-hog

☐ _____
   OTHER

2. Describe your choice in 5 words and write them on the numbered lines.

☆Attention!:
   Do not use the word "cute."

Now, let's make this INTERESTING!

3. Choose a BOLD and completely unrelated word:

☐ Love   ☑ Adventure   ☐ Dawn

☐ _____
   OTHER

4. Write your choice TWICE - on the top and bottom wavy lines.

5. Have a friend do the very same thing on the next page.

☆Attention!:
   Do not show your poem yet!

1 _____

2 _____

3 _____

4 _____

5 _____

POETRY SLAM

Seemingly NONSENSE but Somehow makes so much sense!

1. Choose an animal

☐ mosquito ☐ moose ☐ hedge-hog

☐ _____
            OTHER

2. Describe your choice in 5 words and write them on the numbered lines.

☆ Attention!: Do not use the word "cute."

Now, let's make this INTERESTING!

3. Choose a BOLD and completely unrelated word:

☐ Love ☐ Adventure ☐ Dawn

☐ _____
            OTHER

4. Write your choice TWICE - on the top and bottom wavy lines.

5. Gather an audience and take turns reading your poems out loud and with STYLE! Use rhythm, rap, jazz!

1 _____

2 _____

3 _____

4 _____

5 _____

Drawing with NUMBERS

Draw a flamingo from 2, 3, 4, 6, 11. "Cuckoo?" Go ahead and try it!

Why is the 4 backward? Because the legs of a flamingo bend in the opposite direction of yours.

"ЧТО ЭТО?"
/ShhTOE EH-TUH/
That's RUSSIAN for "What is it?"

~~~~~~~

Well, then...
ЧТО ЭТО?

It's a side view of bacon in a pan.

It's _____ .

It's _____ .

It's _____ .

Take a break. Do something else for 30 minutes.
This will give your mind time to cook up new ideas!
You'll return with a fresh batch of solutions!

It's _____ .

It's _____ .

It's _____ .

Picture This

"An argle-bargle under a bumbershoot"

⇩

/ar-gull bar-gull/
an arguement

⇩

/bum-ber-shoot/
an umbrella

Now draw it!

AGILITY COURSE

Pick up your room to pick up your pace!

→ INSIDE ←

Some movements to consider:
☐ hop ☐ spin ☐ crawl ☐ scoot ☐ _____ OTHER

START

Spin around bear 2 times

On the Wire

Squirrel's best BIRD friends have flown in for a tweet!
There's Tiny, Poofy, Squawky,
HeeHee, King, Genius & Rocket.
Draw them perched on the wires.

Funny how my friends look exactly like their names!

"Was für ein wunderbarer Schnurrbart!"
/ voss fur ine voon·deh·bar·ah shnewerbart /

That's GERMAN for "What a wonderful mustache!"

The RARE & Exotic Scissor Bird

Trace around a pair of scissors to create this squawking fowl.

UnDOODLE it

Turn these doodles into different drawings.

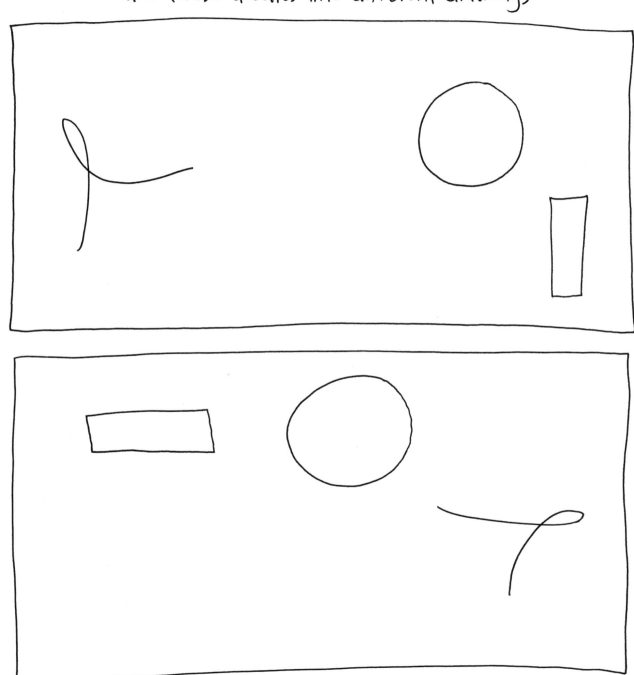

UnDOODLE it

Turn these doodles into different drawings.

Scavenger Hunt: Car Ride

Look for an object that matches the description.
Write down what you find and X what it can fit in.

It can fit in a...

✓ when you see it	DESCRIPTION	What is it?	hand	treasure chest	train car
☐	triangular	_____	☐	☐	☐
☐	striking[1]	_____	☐	☐	☐
☐	dented	_____	☐	☐	☐
☐	purple	_____	☐	☐	☐
☐	furry	_____	☐	☐	☐
☐	noisy	_____	☐	☐	☐
☐	noisome[2]	_____	☐	☐	☐
☐	flashing	_____	☐	☐	☐
☐	amazing	_____	☐	☐	☐
☐	neon	_____	☐	☐	☐

[1] incredible [2] smelly

FONTASTIC

Create a NEW font by redesigning all of the letters of the alphabet.

Ideas for "A"

What will your ABC's look like?

NEW Product for Recess!

What is it? Name it. Label it. Rave about it.

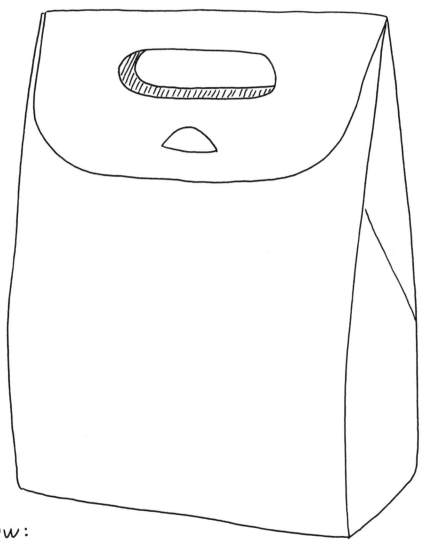

Rave Review:

"Amazing! Ever since I got a carton of _____ , recess
                                        NAME OF PRODUCT

has been ☐ a blast ☐ twice as _____ ☐ _____ !
                                ADJECTIVE   OTHER

Today, I was even able to _____ !"

Picture This

"A NURDLE on the queen's MINIMUS"

⬇

/ner-dull/
a tiny bit of
toothpaste

⬇

/mi-ni-muss/
pinky finger
or pinky toe

Now draw it!

Entrepreneur

→ a person who creates and runs a business

Choose your business:

☐ Walking dogs ☐ Washing windows ☐ Yard work ☐ Organizing

☐ Making & selling art ☐ Giving advice ☐ _____ OTHER

Create a name for your business. Punch it with an adjective:

☐ First-Rate ☐ Amazing ☐ Tip-Top ☐ Finest ☐ _____ OTHER

☆ _____ ☆
Name of Your Business

Design a logo
(the symbol
representing
your business)

List of Supplies: _____

_____

_____

Determine how to charge:

☐ Per job _____ PRICE ☐ Per hour _____ HOURLY FEE ☐ Per item _____ PRICE RANGE

Find customers by creating and...

☐ ... handing out business cards. ☐ ... hanging posters. ☐ ... giving a sales pitch.

Get going!
Fill me up!

"La Petite Poche"

/ law   puh-teet   push (like brush) /

That's FRENCH for "The Little Pocket"
Now draw 12 things that will fit in it!

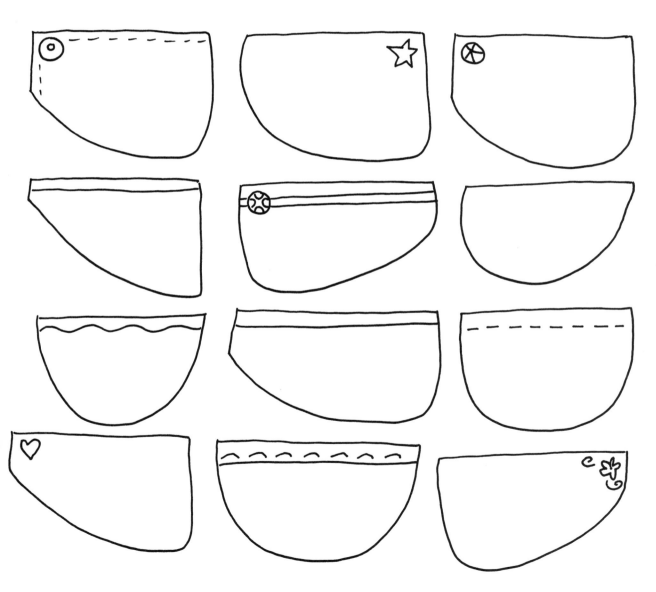

Let's give CUTE a break!
Find NINE new words to describe these cute things.

CAUTION! Entering the territory of a made-up word:

PERSONimate

Personify + Animate

Give human   Make
characteristics   something
to an object   move

Now that you know that... Personimate this:

A Tennis Ball Juggling

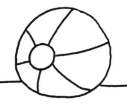

Boomerang: Your Family

What goes around comes around.
So, throw a KINDNESS out there and see what happens!

Your Mission: Think of something SPECIAL you can do for your crew!

Target: _____
Name of Family Members

What will you do?
☐ Pitch In ☐ Entertain ☐ Decorate ☐ _____
other

Details of Your Idea: _____
_____
_____

When will this happen?   Where?
_____   _____

Needed Supplies: _____ Helpers: _____
_____   _____
_____   _____

☆

Your Results: How'd it go?
☐ Fantastic!!! ☐ Terrific!! ☐ Nicely! ☐ _____
other

Explain: _____
_____

How do you feel? ☐ 😊 ☐ 😮 ☐ Motivated ☐ _____
other

WHAT? Where? WHY?
Add details to answer these Qs!

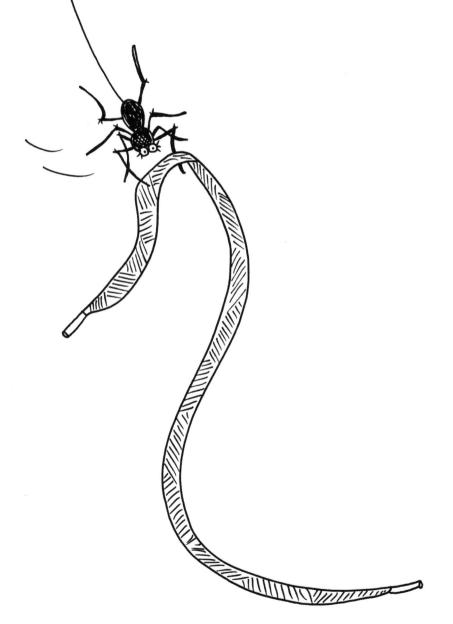

More Grasshoppering!

Jumping from one random idea to another.

I've discovered the best way to stop hiccups is

_____

_____ .

How can you get good luck? _____

_____

_____ .

Where is your favorite hiding spot? _____

WRITE IT TINY

☆ Make a choice and then ask yourself (why?) ☆

☐ canoe or ☐ sailboat   ☐ running or ☐ dancing

☐ future or ☐ past   ☐ Tuesday or ☐ Thursday

☐ spinach or ☐ Brussels sprouts ☐ buying   or ☐ finding
(yes, you must choose one!)   ☐ inside   or ☐ outside

Serve up these options at dinner with a side of "Why?"!

What is possible today? _____

_____

_____

_____

_____

The Tiniest Tourist

"Min hund spiste den!"

/mean hoond spee·steh den/

That's DANISH for "My dog ate it!"

How to draw a furry dog:

ear

HEAD ear

MOUTH BODY TAIL

LEG   LEG

Write down the body parts; then scribble them out.

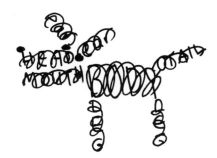

For eyes and nose, add dots.

Draw your own furry dog!

Occasions to use this phrase:
☐ lost homework   ☐ left your cousin's toy in the rain
☐ lost a shoe   ☐ dropped the Thanksgiving turkey
☐ lost a sock   ☐ hid Brussels sprouts in a napkin
☐ ate the last cookie   ☐ _____
                              OTHER

Drawing with: NUMBERS

Draw an angry dog from 3, 6, 8, 9, 11, 0. "Arf'ly hard?" Go ahead and try it!

∞
An "8" on its side is infinity

APPLICATION:
Super Powers

choose your power:

☐ X-ray Vision ☐ Flying ☐ Speed of Cheetah ☐ Incredi-Strength

☐ Underwater Breathing ☐ ESP ☐ _____ OTHER

create a title by choosing a word from each row:

1. ○ Wonder ○ Mega ○ Super ○ Fantastic ○ Amazing

2. ▽ Swift ▽ Strong ▽ Fierce ▽ Bold ▽ _____ OTHER

3. ☐ Kid ☐ Human ☐ Ace ☐ Banana ☐ _____ OTHER

Write your title here: _____ !

I will use my SUPER POWER to:

☐ Help animals ☐ Fight crime ☐ Change the Weather ☐ Entertain

☐ Uncover Secrets ☐ Amaze Friends ☐ Save Nature ☐ _____ OTHER

A typical day with my SUPER POWER:

I wake up and _____

After lunch, I _____

At night, I sometimes _____

Only on Saturdays, I _____

Create a CRITTER

-HONK HONK'- When you are in the CAR, find an object = 🚗 that will fit on this page. Trace around it. Now turn the shape into an OUTRAGEOUS critter.

Which-a-Wayer

Stand up. Walk around looking for a lamp.
Before turning it on, ask the lamp,
"Hey! Do you have any bright ideas?"
Then when you turn it on, exclaim,
"I see that you do! Me too!"

Tell the lamp something you do to brighten up your day:
"I ☐ think up jokes ☐ draw ☐ goof around with friends
☐ practice whistling   ☐ talk to lamps   ☐ gallop
☐ _____   ☐ _____ !"
      OTHER   OTHER

If 💡 seems to be warming up, continue with your conversation:

"You do seem bright! So, tell me the wattage of your bulb.'
  (Find the wattage printed on the light bulb. CAREFUL!)

"I shall ponder the wattage of my own bulb → MY BRAIN!"

By now, the 💡 will want to know your age and zip code.

WHY? To reveal the potential for BIG IDEAS in this particular room!

_____ + _____ + _____ + _____ = _____ !
Light Bulb   Your Brain   Your   Your   Power Wattage
 Wattage   Wattage   Age   Zip Code   for BIG IDEAS

What's on the Surface?

NEW Product for Time Travel!
What is it? Name it. Label it. Rave about it.

Time Travel HAIR

Rave Review:

"Wow! I traveled ☐15 ☐50 ☐ OTHER Years into the ☐future ☐past!

I visited _____ in _____
            NAME OF PERSON   PLACE

and found out _____!
                  COOL FACT (YOU CAN MAKE IT UP!)

Which-a-Wayer

Stand up. Tiptoe your age in any direction.
Close your eyes and spin around singing the ABCs.

When you get to z, freeze and point.
Now guess what you're pointing at. Open your eyes.

Are you right? If yes, draw a picture of it.
If no, try again!

UnDOODLE it

Turn these doodles into different drawings.

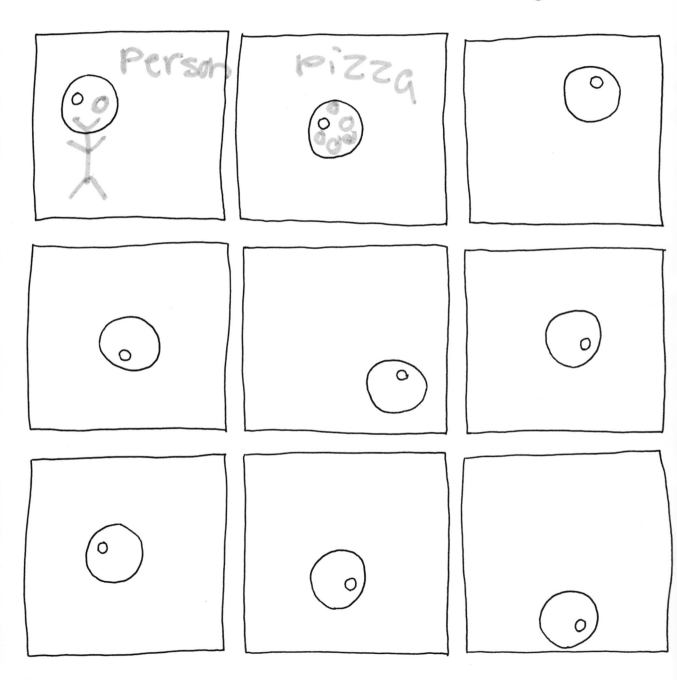

FOR YOU! ☆ POETRY SLAM ⚡

Seemingly NONSENSE but Somehow makes so much sense!

1. Choose a body of water:

☐ ocean ☐ river ☐ fountain

☐ _____
       OTHER

2. Describe your choice in 5 words and write them on the numbered lines.

☆ Attention!: Do not use the word "wet."

Now, let's make this INTERESTING!

3. Choose a BOLD and completely unrelated word:

☐ Peace ☐ Justice ☐ Courage

☐ _____
       OTHER

4. Write your choice TWICE - on the top and bottom wavy lines.

5. Have a friend do the very same thing on the next page.

☆ Attention!: Do not show your poem yet!

1 _____

2 _____

3 _____

4 _____

5 _____

For a FRIEND! ☆ POETRY SLAM

Seemingly NONSENSE but Somehow makes so much sense!

1. Choose a body of water:

☑ ocean ☐ river ☐ fountain

☐ _____
　　　　 OTHER

2. Describe your choice in 5 words and write them on the numbered lines.
☆ Attention!:
　 Do not use the word "wet."

Now, let's make this INTERESTING!

3. Choose a BOLD and completely unrelated word:

☑ Peace ☐ Justice ☐ Courage

☐ _____
　　　　 OTHER

4. Write your choice TWICE - on the top and bottom wavy lines.

5. Gather an audience and take turns reading your poems out loud and with STYLE! Use rhythm, rap, jazz!

1 _____

2 _____

3 _____

4 _____

5 _____

Create a CRITTER

Go OUTSIDE. Find a bit of nature that will fit on this page. Trace around it. Now turn the shape into a Mysterious critter.

"O que é isso?"
/OKAY A EE-SO/
That's PORTUGUESE for "What is it?"

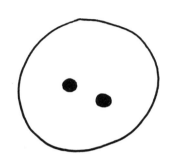

Hmm? Then...
O que é isso?

It's two raisins in the bottom of a cup.

It's a face that only has eyes for you!

It's _____.

It's _____.

It's _____.

My parent thinks it's _____.

My friend thinks it's _____.

My other friend thinks it's _____.

Actually, it could be _____.

A Pyramid of Fish

Scavenger Hunt: Kitchen

Look for an object that matches the description.
Write down what you find and X what it can fit in.

It can fit in a...

✓ when you see it	DESCRIPTION	What is it?	hand	treasure chest	train car
☐	round	_____	☐	☐	☐
☐	silver	_____	☐	☐	☐
☐	perishable[1]	_____	☐	☐	☐
☐	polka-dotted	_____	☐	☐	☐
☐	pliant[2]	_____	☐	☐	☐
☐	sticky	_____	☐	☐	☐
☐	opaque[3]	_____	☐	☐	☐
☐	out of reach	_____	☐	☐	☐
☐	aromatic[4]	_____	☐	☐	☐
☐	heavy	_____	☐	☐	☐

[1] could rot [2] bendable [3] not clear [4] having a nice smell

84

Drawing with Letters:

Draw a mouse from J, U, X, M, K, S. "Eek!" Go ahead and try it!

Mice tails can grow as long as their bodies. Imagine if the same were true for you if you had a tail!

"Appyhay Irthdaybay!"
/appy·hay   irthday·bay/
That's PIG LATIN for "Happy Birthday!"

Say more!
Take the first consonant(s) and move it to the end. Add "ay."
If a word begins with a vowel, just add "way" to the end.
Get it?! = Etgay itway?!

Happy birthday!

Design
a party,
for a pig!
checklist:
☐ akecay
☐ alloonsbay
☐ artypay
   at-hay

Picture This

"A SNOLLYGASTER shouting, "GARDYLOO!""

/snaw-lee-gas-ter/

⇩

a clever and
deceitful person

/gar-dee-loo/

⇩

a warning shouted
before throwing
water from above

Now draw it!

Rippling

"Please continue on with my cuckoo pattern!"

WHAT? Where? WHY?
Add details to answer these Qs!

Boomerang: Neighborhood

What goes around comes around.
So, throw a KINDNESS out there and see what happens!

Your Mission: Think of something GREAT you can do for your 'hood!

Target: _____
                Neighborhood or Street Name

What will you do?
☐ Clean Up   ☐ Brighten   ☐ Organize an Event   ☐ _____
                                                     other
Details of your Idea: _____

_____

_____

When will this happen?   Where?

_____   _____

Needed Supplies: _____   Helpers: _____

_____   _____

_____   _____

Your Results: How'd it go?
☐ Even better than I imagined!!!   ☐ GREAT!   ☐ Pretty Good!
Explain: _____

_____

How do you feel? ☐ ☺ ☐ Wowza! ☐ ☆ ☐ _____
                                            other

CAUTION! Entering the territory of a made-up word:

PERSONimate

Personify + Animate
Give human   Make
characteristics   something
to an object   move

Now that you know that... Personimate this:

Two Cupcakes Jumping Rope

◖Ε C●d◗e

Hidden in the house are angles, arcs, and wiggles.
Each one represents a pair of letters.
If the shape includes a "•", select the second letter.
For example: ⌐ ⌐ = Hi!

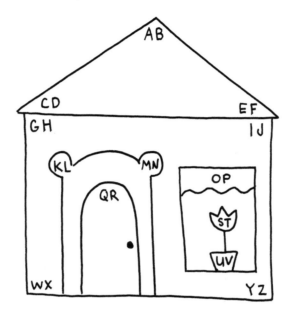

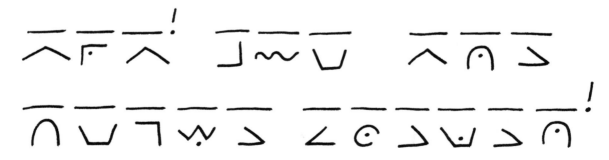

Look in a mirror. Lock eyes with the person who appears.
Shout out what you've just decoded!
Repeat pointing your finger this time for greater effect!

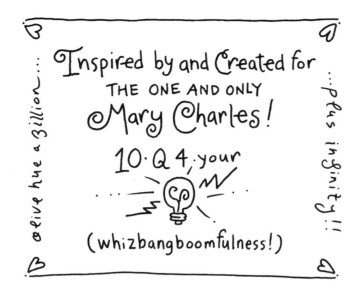

Inspired by and Created for
THE ONE AND ONLY
Mary Charles!
10·Q 4, your
(whizbangboomfulness!)

olive hue a Billion...

...plus infinity!!

DREAM IT! DRAW IT! THINK IT! DO IT!

Andrews McMeel Publishing
a division of Andrews McMeel Universal
1130 Walnut Street, Kansas City, Missouri 64106
www.andrewsmcmeel.com

16 17 18 19 20 TEN 10 9 8 7 6 5 4 3 2 1

ISBN: 978-1-4494-8034-9

Editor: Jean Z. Lucas
Designer: Diane Marsh
Art Director: Diane Marsh
Production Editor: Maureen Sullivan
Production Manager: Tamara Haus

Made by: 1010 Printing International, Ltd.
Address and place of production:
1010 Avenue, Xia Nan Industrial District,
Yuan Zhou Town, Bo Luo County
Guang Don Province, China 516123
1st printing – 7/15/16

ATTENTION: SCHOOLS AND BUSINESSES
Andrews McMeel books are available at quantity discounts with bulk purchase for educational, business, or sales promotional use. For information, please e-mail the Andrews McMeel Publishing Special Sales Department: specialsales@amuniversal.com.

COLLECT
THESE
FUN BOOKS
IN THE
GO FUN!
SERIES

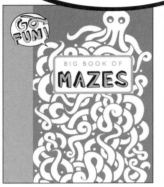

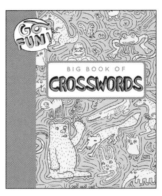

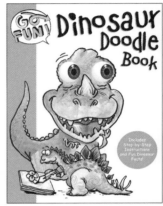

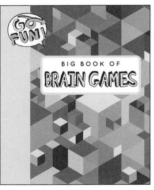

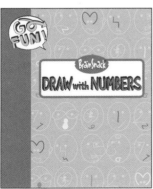

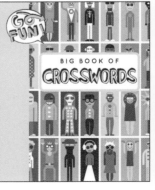

Back
in
15!